BUNGALOW STYLE

ARCHITECTURE & DESIGN LIBRARY

BUNGALOW STYLE

April Halberstadt

FRIEDMAN/FAIRFAX
PUBLISHERS

A FRIEDMAN/FAIRFAX BOOK

Friedman/Fairfax Publishers

15 West 26 Street

New York, NY 10010

Telephone (212) 685-6610

Fax (212) 685-1307

Please visit our website: www.metrobooks.com

Library of Congress Cataloging-in-Publication Data available upon request.

ISBN 1-56799-783-X

Editor: Reka Simonsen

Art Director: Jeff Batzli

Designer: Jennifer Markson

Photography Editor: Sarah Storey

Production Manager: Richela Fabian

Color separations by Colourscan Pte. Ltd.

Printed in Hong Kong by Midas Printing Co. Ltd.

3 5 7 9 10 8 6 4 2

Distributed by Sterling Publishing Co., Inc.

387 Park Avenue South

New York, NY 10016-8810

Orders and customer service (800) 367-9692

Fax: (800) 542-7567

E-mail: custservice@sterlingpub.com

Website: www.sterlingpublishing.com

To Maeve Hope Horton, my sister and first playmate.

I am especially grateful for the enthusiasm and support of Marti Wachtel, Charles and Veronica Ensor, Chris and Stephanie Hope, David and Sarah Halberstadt, and my husband Hans Halberstadt. All helped out on this project . . . I couldn't have done it without you!

C o n t e n t s

INTRODUCTION

It was a dark and rainy night in March during the early 1970s when I first saw the bungalow that is now my home. My first encounter was memorable and not especially pleasant. We wanted a large, comfortable Victorian-era house, but our broker had dragged us to any suburban structure more than thirty years old that he thought might appeal to us. After touring several of his selections, I was prepared for another wild goose chase. Distracted by squirmy children, stormy weather, and the broker's chatter, we did not examine the house carefully. We made our bid after looking at the house with flashlights.

The next day, we drove back to see what we had done. The bungalow had been built in 1909, but the style seemed ageless. It wasn't Victorian, but it did have a great deal of appeal. I felt very comfortable as I moved from room to room. Its most obvious exterior feature was a porch that covered the entire front of the house, wrapping around the side to the main entrance. There was enough room here for a porch swing, maybe even two.

We bought the house and made immediate plans to update and upgrade the interior. The woodwork was nice but a little strange, I thought, so I planned to modify it as soon as possible with some interesting Victorian-style details. The picture-rail moldings were not elaborate and the leaded glass was definitely on the plain side. To my uneducated eye, the place really needed some Victorian embellishment. It took a long time before I understood the quiet restraint of bungalow style.

As I became familiar with my new neighborhood, I noticed nearby houses with similar styling and details. I did not realize it until many years later, but I was just one of many who were becoming fascinated by bungalows. I looked for any scrap of information about these small houses. I was amazed to discover that they were first built at the turn of the century, since they felt so contemporary to me.

It's been going on for more than two decades now, an intense resurgence of interest in a wonderful style of North American housing

OPPOSITE: *A contemporary interpretation of a bungalow entry shows the influence of the Japanese detailing that has become part of the bungalow aesthetic. The style calls for restraint and for a partnership with the natural beauty of the landscape. The porch supports and detailing of the eaves recall the simplicity of the Japanese* tori *(spirit) gate.*

commonly called the Craftsman bungalow. Architectural historians still debate the origin and development of the earliest bungalows, but this style of housing, a product of the American Arts and Crafts Movement, seems to have appeared before the turn of the twentieth century and become almost instantly popular.

The American Arts and Crafts Movement was a well-documented artistic philosophy at the turn of the century, with many publications and periodicals discussing its ideals and aesthetics. One of the most famous periodicals was *The Craftsman*, a beautiful magazine designed and written by Gustav Stickley to promote his furniture designs. Stickley soon incorporated bungalow floor plans and designs into the magazine and began to sell the house plans by mail. Other magazines followed suit, and bungalows began to appear across North America.

Today, bungalow style is considered one of the largest components of the American Arts and Crafts Movement. This movement emphasized the importance of the individual craftsperson, creating a social order in which the worker was not enslaved by a machine but enjoyed his or her work. Architectural plans, furniture, textiles, and decorative objects were lovingly produced by skilled artisans for their beauty and utility. The Arts and Crafts Movement was more than just a style of furniture and a political philosophy; it was a search for the greater meaning of life through art and nature. The focus was on living life as an

RIGHT: *Bungalow style can easily be reinterpreted for contemporary living. The deep overhanging eaves, the use of natural materials, and the siting of the house within a wooded area are timeless bungalow design elements. The golden color of this bungalow blends beautifully with the autumn leaves. The rich hue is due to the fact that the siding is new, but the house will still be handsome and well suited to the landscape when the wood has weathered to a silvery gray.*

expression of the inner self; the house and its furnishings only sup-ported the search for a deeper understanding of the relationship with one's own spirit. And so the bungalow became the ultimate artifact in the search for spiritual understanding.

As we arrive at the turn of another century and examine our roots, it's fascinating to see that the artistic expressions of our ideals have come full circle. The bungalow style, with its emphasis on the appreci-ation of simple goodness, living in harmony with nature, and striving for excellence in craftsmanship, is timely once again.

ABOVE: *The place where the family gathers in a bungalow home is meant to be comfortable and cozy. The furnishings should reflect the craftsmanship local to the area, such as the handwoven rug, willow basket, and handmade lampshades in this Southwestern-style living room. Even the window coverings should be simple, like these woven linen shades.*

ABOVE: *Living as one with nature is a bungalow ideal, beautifully expressed in this upstairs room that opens onto a wonderful treetop view. The armchair and sidechair are fine examples of the simple, heavy oak pieces that Gustav Stickley popularized.*

ABOVE: *The architectural team of Henry and Charles Greene brought bungalow design to a high art. In the entry hallway of the Gamble house in Pasadena, California, the furnishings are completely integrated with the interior spaces. Heavily influenced by Japanese art, the Greene brothers designed the house as well as all of the furnishings and details, including the lighting and the leaded-glass windows.*

ABOVE: *A completely integrated environment, indoors and out, was the goal of bungalow designers.*
Fireplaces made of river rock, such as this rugged example, are typical features in vintage bungalows.
A variety of houseplants continues the nature theme indoors, and a collection of art pottery adds color.

CHAPTER ONE

HOUSES IN THE LANDSCAPE

A century after its introduction, bungalow living is immensely popular with a new generation of home-owner. Perhaps this is because bungalows are con-structed of natural materials from renewable resources, which fits so well with the contemporary ideal of living lightly on the land. Perhaps this renaissance is due to an appreciation of bungalow craftsmanship and the quality of construction. Or perhaps bungalow living is appealing because of its deep philosophic roots: the idea that art, spirit, and nature are one.

The appearance of the bungalow at the beginning of the twentieth century went hand in hand with a prolonged period of North American prosperity and an accompanying building boom from coast to coast. Bungalow construction also coincided with the evolution of the street-car suburbs, those housing developments just outside an urban center that were served by electric railroads or trolley lines. It was the ideal house for the new suburbs. Away from the demands of formal town life, with the social requirements of parlors, calling cards, and at-home days, the bungalow was designed to be managed without servants.

Suitable for both rural and urban locales, the bungalow was the house with the best of both worlds. It offered the peaceful charm of country life and the labor-saving conveniences of a modern home. Perhaps the most predominant style of housing built between 1900 and 1930, bungalows are found all across the United States and Canada. They continued to be built in large numbers until first the Great Depression and then World War II put building construction on hold.

There are many stylistic variations on the basic bungalow theme. A bungalow is a single-story residence with a wide porch or verandah, a roof with generous eaves that shade the windows from summer sun, and an open floor plan. While a general feature of the style is to have all the living areas on one floor, many bungalows were built with sleep-ing rooms on a second floor. Early building permits describe these as "story-and-a-half," perhaps because the upstairs rooms fit cozily under the eaves, within the framing of the rafters.

OPPOSITE: *It's easy to see why the little bungalow became the most popular style of housing built in North America between 1900 and World War II. With proper maintenance, many of these houses have lasted nearly a century and their charm is as enduring as their construction.*

Bungalows have been built with details to suit every taste. Some have the half-timbering reminiscent of Tudor styling, while some have the shutters and window boxes of a Swiss chalet. Still other bungalows have tile roofs, constructed with imitation Spanish tile formed of lead to create a "mission" look.

Simplicity of line and detail is an important bungalow characteristic. In contrast to the fussy ornamentation of Victorian cottages, bungalows often rely upon the careful placement of simply framed windows to add visual interest to their facades. While Victorian homes are generally painted and decorated both inside and out, bungalows are made of local materials that need no paint, and age beautifully. The bungalow embraces sunshine, wind, and rain, using the natural weathering of the materials as a design element. Stone, river rocks, naturally rough and unevenly colored clinker bricks, and cedar or redwood shakes and shingles are frequently found on exterior surfaces.

The Arts and Crafts emphasis on natural materials used simply and appropriately for the environment produced houses that reflected their locales. Bungalows in the colder northern and eastern regions are often built of brick and stone and feature enclosed porches and large fireplaces with cozy inglenooks. The bungalows built in the West and the Southwest generally have plank, shingle, or stucco exteriors and the porches remain open for outdoor living and dining. The marriage of house and site, of form and function, of spirit and purpose produced a style of residential architecture that is truly adaptable, and at once modern and traditional.

RIGHT: *The river rock used for the porch and chimney of this bungalow has been carefully chosen and installed so that the subtle color variations in the rocks form a random and attractive pattern. Although bungalow design is frequently restrained, a careful observer can soon spot the loving details that make these houses so special.*

LEFT: *Bungalow style welcomes visitors, bringing them immediately into a warm and comfortable place. This generously proportioned front door with its heavy, hand-forged hinges proudly declares the owners' appreciation of the craftsman's hand.*

RIGHT, TOP:

Craftsman bungalows frequently feature the lavish use of local materials weathered to a beautiful patina. The approach to this home's entry is actually quite formal, but the texture of the stone stairway and the abundant greenery create a sense of welcome.

RIGHT, BOTTOM:

These Midwestern bungalows have been given a new lease on life. With a glorious paint scheme and colorful landscaping, this is now a small business park, filled with comfortable bungalows refitted especially for today's small consulting businesses that have just a few employees.

OPPOSITE: *Natural stone is the most prominent material used in this contemporary home, which borrows much from the philosophy of the bungalow. The long, low veranda that runs nearly the entire length of the house, the posts that are left unpainted to weather naturally, and the generous use of stone all mirror the Craftsman philosophy.*

ABOVE: *A stairway and partial walls of dark red brick create a dramatic and unusual entrance to this shingled bungalow. The wooden doorway and the darker plank eaves of the overhang are a good illustration of the influence that Japanese design had on bungalow style. Native plants, such as low-growing cypress trees and vibrant orange California poppies, have been chosen for the garden.*

LEFT: *Nearly obscured by the surrounding shrubs, this bungalow appears small from the outside but is actually quite spacious. Although many bungalows look like single-story houses, there are frequently four or more upstairs rooms tucked away under the eaves. The old building permits sometimes refer to these houses as "story-and-a-half," but despite the connotation, the upstairs bedrooms are usually generously sized.*

OPPOSITE: *A bungalow in a forest setting almost always features shingles, in this case the wonderful redwood shingles that are probably a common material in this locale. The builder has omitted the low overhanging eaves more common on bungalows in sunnier climates, since sunlight is a precious commodity in wooded areas, but the wide porch remains a prominent feature.*

ABOVE: *Bungalow style remains very popular today because it has such universal appeal. Here, the architect used the pattern and rhythm of the window openings to create architectural interest, a design idea common in later bungalows. Porches are an even more prominent feature here than on a traditional bungalow: note the small open porch along the front of the house, the larger screened porch at the end, and the little one on the second floor that offers a wonderful view of the scenery.*

ABOVE: *This vintage bungalow, with its sand-colored shingles and tidy white trim, was built before World War I. Tall river rock and wooden pillars support a narrow porch that wraps around two sides of the home. The thin wooden slats can be used as a pergola for climbing vines during the warm months, but even bare, they provide shade and make this porch a comfortable place to sit and enjoy the sights and scents of the flowers in the front yard.*

A B O V E : *This single-story home effectively unites the indoors and the outdoors. When all of the doors are open, the residents are part of the landscape. The natural, unpainted wood siding, the decorative use of stone, and the very simple detailing of the windows are a contemporary expression of bungalow ideals.*

RIGHT: *This bungalow from Naglee Park in San Jose, California, was built around 1910. Fussy Victorian detailing was abandoned in favor of the simple yet still intricate carpentry work evident in the eaves of this home.*

BELOW: *A bungalow has an intimate relationship with its landscape, and this charming example features a pergola that wraps itself around the front windows to provide support for an assortment of vines. Light and air are essential to bungalow living, and the many generously sized windows of this little house invite the outdoors inside.*

ABOVE: *The generous use of river rock, carefully installed and laid by a master craftsman, makes this bungalow stand out in its California neighborhood, where most bungalows are built completely of wood. The unusual porch on this house is another element that sets it apart, since much of it is open to the elements rather than protected by an overhang.*

ABOVE: *Designer Marti Wachtel re-created the facade of this bungalow in the Rose Garden district of San Jose, California. The entry porch is entirely new, modeled after a classic bungalow, and helps rejuvenate the old house, which had been badly "modernized." The old gray concrete sidewalk has been covered with warm brick.*

OPPOSITE: *Bright autumn leaves bring their own kind of beauty to the yard of this bungalow. The tall shrubs surrounding the porch provide greenery all year long, but no effort has been made to fight the seasons with non-native plants that would bloom even in winter. Part of the bungalow aesthetic is that the house should be in harmony with nature.*

OPPOSITE: *Porches are among the most important characteristics of the bungalow, frequently covering two sides of the house. Plain architectural details, such as these square pillars and the simple geometric balustrade, are in keeping with the clean, pared-down aesthetic of bungalow style. The landscaping is casual, surrounding the house with natural beauty.*

RIGHT, TOP: *Sitting in the fresh air for part of every day was considered an important part of a healthy lifestyle at the beginning of the twentieth century, so bungalows promoted a special relationship with the outdoors. Many bungalows feature a secluded corner or sheltered sun porch that allows one to enjoy the sunshine, especially during the darker winter months. This charming bungalow has both, as well as a small deck that provides a spot for alfresco meals.*

RIGHT, BOTTOM: *Bungalow style places a special emphasis on living with nature, bringing the outdoors inside the home. This appealing window box provides a bridge between the garden and a cozy life inside. A window box works well for viewers indoors and out, providing a charming focal point for both the residents and the passersby.*

CHAPTER TWO

INNER SPACES, INNER SPIRIT

At the beginning of the twentieth century, the new bungalow style expressed new ideas about the importance of family life. As poet Charles Keeler described the interior, "It is to be used, lived in, made a part and expression of the family circle." The hearth was highly romanticized and considered the heart of the home. The family was encouraged to gather around the glow of the fireplace in the evening, to read or listen to stories from great literature and to discuss great ideas.

The bungalow was designed with an emphasis on living a healthful, wholesome life. Fussy, stuffy Victorian houses with their rigid floor plans and emphasis on formal etiquette were rejected for more open and practical homes that encouraged greater casual interaction. The bungalow did away with the boxed-in rooms of its predecessors and relied instead on flowing interior spaces, sometimes incorporating a "room within a room" by defining an area with rug placement and furniture groupings. Today's renovations often echo the original bungalow design by moving or eliminating walls to combine rooms for increased openness. Even in smaller homes, the open layout conveys a feeling of spaciousness.

A cozy, warm entry welcomes friends and family members. The living areas of the bungalow are arranged for the comfort and convenience of the family, rather than to impress visitors. Woodwork in the living rooms is commonly pine, fir, or other softwood, either varnished or left natural. Flooring is frequently oak and sometimes maple in the family rooms, while floors in bedrooms and rooms that receive little foot traffic are usually of fir or other softwood. If the center of the room features a piece of Wilton carpet or a Native American rug, the covered area is commonly made of pine or fir, with the exposed perimeter surfaced with hardwood.

OPPOSITE: *This dining room is filled with handsome wooden architectural details, such as the window frames, decorative ceiling beams, and the sideboard and cabinets that are built into the wall. Built-ins are a common bungalow feature, since they are especially useful in small homes. Like all elements of the design style, they are beautiful as well as functional, often sporting leaded- or stained-glass doors.*

Woodwork in the bedrooms, nursery, and bathrooms is usually painted white or a pastel hue. Bedrooms emphasize lightness and airiness, so white or soft colors are preferred. Beds in a traditional bungalow are often of oak, simply and solidly constructed. Dressers and nightstands frequently retain their natural wood finishes and sport gracefully geometric metal hardware. Sheer curtains let in plenty of natural light; after dark, mica-shaded lamps give the room a rich, cozy glow. Straightforward metal beds and pale-hued wicker furnishings work equally well in the bungalow bedroom, perhaps paired with crisp off-white linens and an unfussy stained-glass lamp. A few embroidered accent pillows add a touch of color and pattern.

Bathrooms are fresh and clean-looking, with porcelain or enamel fixtures, and white tile acting as wainscoting. Floors are generally covered with small octagonal tiles in white or sometimes black, blue, or dark green. The bathroom was a relatively new luxury when bungalows were first built, so many original owners were content with small, simple bathrooms. Today, owners often expand them into luxurious spaces for personal pampering, incorporating additional colors and materials. As with furnishings in the rest of the house, oak or other wooden cabinetry works well in the bathroom.

The kitchen underwent drastic changes at the turn of the century as improvements in technology and an understanding of the importance of sanitation in food preparation became widespread. The bungalow kitchen is often a suite of rooms, each devoted to a particular aspect of domestic management. Bungalows built for the well-to-do may have a butler's pantry in addition to the main cooking area, used primarily for storing tableware and linens. The term "butler's pantry" is a charming misnomer, since few North American households at the time employed more than a "day lady" for domestic help. Smaller bungalows generally feature a kitchen with a single pantry and utility area. For convenience, many bungalows have a window or pass-through between the kitchen and dining room so food may be served easily.

Linoleum, made of compressed sawdust and linseed oil and available in dozens of colors and patterns, was widely used in kitchen and bathroom areas. Modern sheet-vinyl flooring can be readily found in patterns echoing these period styles, as can decorative tiles for use as accents on the backsplash or countertop. Tiles made of slate or other natural materials also work well.

Although bungalow kitchens were frequently small, both to foster economy of movement and because they had few space-hungry appliances, it is possible to renovate the kitchen and still retain the period flavor. The open kitchen plan so popular nowadays is very much in keeping with the general layout of a bungalow-style home, and the clean lines of modern stainless steel appliances can blend beautifully with Arts and Crafts detailing. When a fuller renovation is not possible, consider workable options such as incorporating natural woods by introducing freestanding pieces, refacing the existing cabinets, or simply changing the hardware to introduce period detailing.

OPPOSITE: *Many architects of the Arts and Crafts Movement preferred the natural beauty of wood for bungalow interiors. The abundant use of rich, dark wood in this handsome living room makes the space both elegant and comfortable. The beauty of the natural environment outdoors is highlighted by the decorative frieze of birch trees painted above the wainscot.*

OPPOSITE: *Although the decor is contemporary, this cozy bungalow kitchen takes its cue from the Arts and Crafts ideal of living in harmony with nature. The surface of the cabinets has been left untreated so that the rugged grain of the wood is visible. Wicker baskets act as drawers to store kitchen utensils, and herbs and vines grow everywhere, even above the window and along the hanging light fixture.*

ABOVE: *The bungalow kitchen is a working kitchen, sometimes opening onto a pantry or a scullery. At the time that most bungalows were built, sanitation was heavily emphasized, so bungalow kitchens have surfaces that are easy to clean. This sunny kitchen has the painted woodwork typical of the era.*

ABOVE: *In the early twentieth century, eating in the kitchen was considered to be a lower-class practice, so bungalows of the period generally have either a dining room or a breakfast room— and sometimes both—adjacent to the kitchen. The bungalow-era kitchen has been beautifully interpreted here, with an emphasis on the simplicity and warmth that are hallmarks of the style.*

ABOVE: *Oak cabinetry in the Arts and Crafts tradition creates a warm and simple atmosphere. While many bungalow kitchens have white painted cupboards, since these were thought to be sanitary, others feature simple, well-designed cabinets in oak or fir.*

OPPOSITE: *The traditional bungalow kitchen was a model of cleanliness, with tiled walls and countertops and white cabinetry. This kitchen is a loving re-creation of typical Depression-era decor, from the period appliances, tiled walls, and all-white scheme to the stylized Chinese red pottery and steel drawer pulls.*

RIGHT: *A high, white ceiling, numerous lamps, and large windows make this simple kitchen wonderfully light and airy, which was a goal of traditional bungalow style. This contemporary galley kitchen successfully applies the bungalow aesthetic to modern life.*

LEFT: *The bungalow arrived during an era when modern conveniences such as indoor plumbing and gas stoves were becoming a standard part of North American life. Although this bungalow kitchen has been updated with a contemporary stove and recessed lighting, the Craftsman-style worktable, along with the traditional cabinet design and pulls, recalls the Arts and Crafts era.*

ABOVE: *The bungalow kitchen was supposed to be a comfortable work space with plenty of room and light. This kitchen has a spacious quality, thanks to the open floor plan and the careful design of the cooking area. The extensive use of cupboards painted in a pale color and the bank of windows make it a pleasant place to cook.*

ABOVE: *The hearth is traditionally the center of the bungalow home, the place where the family gathers to read, play games, and talk. This unique fireplace is raised off the floor and has a convenient granite ledge in front that takes the place of a side table. The dining table is nearby for cozy meals lighted by candles and the glow of the fire.*

ABOVE: *Naturally finished wood indoors and treetops outdoors turn this room into a cozy, peaceful space for meals and meetings. The ceiling light fixture is of a design that was quite popular in the Arts and Crafts era, intended to create atmosphere in the room rather than to supply an optimal amount of light.*

ABOVE: *This contemporary home incorporates and even updates many elements from traditional bungalow style. The numerous windows are divided with simple sashing that adds drama to the architecture, as do the soaring exposed ceiling beams. Reproductions of classic Stickley-style furnishings fill the room, and the elegant lamps are an updated version of a typical Arts and Crafts design.*

RIGHT: *The bungalow style is sometimes considered the first real American design style, with an emphasis on the work of local craftsmen and the use of regional materials. Bungalows have had a great influence on contemporary home design, which also focuses on rooms that share light, space, and function. Decorative details, such as quilts, homespun-style fabrics, and naturally finished wood, contribute to the bungalow feeling of this contemporary house.*

ABOVE: *The preferred fabrics and decorative items in a bungalow house are those that emphasize a relationship with nature. Here the furniture is dressed with simple canvas covers, the floor with sisal matting, and the pillows with handwoven fabric in Native American designs. All the design elements encouraged by the Arts and Crafts ideal are exemplified in this contemporary living room, which has the airy, outdoorsy quality of a porch.*

ABOVE: *The open floor plan of the bungalow allows one space to flow into another, seemingly without walls. This inviting sunroom provides natural light as well as a beautiful view for the rooms in the middle of the house. Simple, carefully chosen furnishings contribute to the inviting ambience.*

LEFT: *The Greene brothers were noted for their intricate furniture designs, which were influenced by their interest in Japanese art. This living room illustrates all the elements of the bungalow style: a completely integrated design, a warm and light atmosphere, and abundant evidence of the craftsman's hand in the furniture, art pottery, and light fixtures.*

ABOVE: *Charles Keeler, a poet and lecturer of the Arts and Crafts Movement, promoted the ideal room as one that created "an atmosphere." He recommended warm colors such as buff or tan, and rooms full of warmth and brightness. In this period-perfect room, the furnishings, surface treatments, and accessories are integrated in color and scale, creating a space that is comfortable and restful.*

ABOVE: *Many bungalow houses have one room that was intended to be used for open-air sleeping, even in winter weather, since closed, heated rooms were believed to foster tuberculosis. This bedroom has a warm and cozy feeling, thanks to the rich wood used from floor to ceiling, but the plentiful windows ensure that the sleeper has enough fresh air.*

RIGHT: *Furniture designed for the bungalow was simple and frequently made of rattan, wicker, or bamboo. This lovely bedroom has been decorated in period style, with wicker chairs and chaises, a clean-lined brass bedstead, and soft, sheer curtains at the window.*

OPPOSITE: *After the heavy velvets and dust-catching ruffled draperies of the Victorian era, bungalow furnishings were kept as simple as possible for both aesthetic and sanitary reasons. Clean lines and light colors are still popular for bungalow bedrooms, since their understated quality is so well suited to the architecture.*

RIGHT, TOP: *Traditionally, bedroom furnishings were kept to a minimum and light, cool colors were used. This simplicity is still one of the best options for a bungalow bedroom, since it creates a sense of airiness and peace that is ideal. This bedroom needs nothing more than a handsome wooden bed with sheer curtains and a bouquet of garden roses to become a sanctuary.*

RIGHT, BOTTOM: *This contemporary interpretation of the bungalow style follows the tenets of the Arts and Crafts Movement by bringing nature indoors, keeping the lines of the furniture simple, and eliminating all unnecessary clutter. The pale colors and abundant natural light also recall that era.*

LEFT: *Claw-foot tubs have proven to be so popular that many contemporary manufacturers have started to produce them. Tiled wainscoting on the walls around the tub is a frequent period detail, and it is used to good effect in this slightly updated bungalow bathroom.*

OPPOSITE: *The bungalow was the first housing style to combine all the plumbing in one room. This bathroom is a blend of modern and turn-of-the-century elements, from the contemporary toilet to the period-style pedestal sink. The neutral palette and garden theme add to the vintage feeling.*

ABOVE: *Updating a century-old bathroom always poses special problems for the renovator. What can be saved and what has to be replaced? This bathroom, a successful blend of old and new elements, has many features typical of the Craftsman era: the toilet and pedestal sink, the painted wainscoting, and decorative details such as the lamps and mirror.*

ABOVE, LEFT: *The craftsman's hand is often evident in the interior finishes of bungalow houses. Handcrafted tiles and untreated wooden cabinets are expressions of the creativity that was especially valued by early devotees of the Arts and Crafts Movement. The simple stained-glass windows and period light fixtures are also evocative of bungalow style.*

ABOVE, RIGHT: *Bungalow-era bathrooms emphasize cleanliness and sanitation, important concepts in the early twentieth century, when the knowledge of germs was relatively recent. A vintage wooden sink cabinet and period light fixtures, typical of those found in a bungalow home, create the atmosphere in this bath.*

CHAPTER THREE

THE BUNGALOW AESTHETIC

William Morris, one of the spiritual leaders of the Arts and Crafts Movement said, "Have nothing in your house that is not functional or that you do not believe to be beautiful." The Arts and Crafts Movement was founded on the ideal that the individual artisan should be celebrated. This philosophy of design integrity covered every aspect of bungalow style. Furniture and carpets, curtains and table linens, dishes and cutlery were all thoughtfully designed and carefully produced. The decorative arts were also reconsidered, and the design philosophy applied to painting, jewelry, and fine metalwork, as well as art glass and pottery.

The Arts and Crafts Movement was the dawn of the era when interior designers began to be noted as artists in their own right. These designers had an ability to provide a unified theme to their decors. From the carpets and curtains to the furniture and light fixtures, every aspect of the well-appointed bungalow was chosen for its simplicity and beauty. This was the era when the dictum "form follows function" first appeared. The beauty of an object rose from its usefulness.

Bungalow furniture is simple, handsome, and solidly constructed of oak or occasionally fir. Lines are clean and devoid of overembellishment. Above all, the furniture design is inspired by nature, with motifs based on organic forms and with the natural grain of the wood used as part of the decoration. While collectors prize the trademarked pieces produced by the Roycroft or Stickley studios, many furnishings from the era have no markings. Mission-style furniture, as it was sometimes called, was widely imitated by many furniture makers from east to west. Simple wooden furnishings of almost any era complement the bungalow aesthetic, as do pieces crafted from other natural materials such as wicker, rattan, or leather.

No matter what the general decor of a bungalow, bungalow owners today seem to prefer lamps and lighting fixtures in the Craftsman style. Hanging fixtures made of pierced metal or colored glass are often placed on porches or over dining tables. Table lamps are frequently made of hammered metal with simple shades of vellum or mica. Today's bungalow owner is extremely creative with lighting sources for the home, since few really functional original lighting fixtures are available from the era. Fortunately, a number of manufacturers

OPPOSITE: *Rugged stone and polished wood bring the spirit of bungalow style into this contemporary home. The large, irregular stones of the fireplace are softened and made elegant with a dark wooden split mantel that is reminiscent of the work of Charles Rennie Mackintosh, an important architect and designer of the Arts and Crafts Movement.*

William Morris papers or other appropriate patterns. Wooden walls are often left untreated to allow their beauty to shine, or walls may be painted in soft, natural colors, since neutral backgrounds are ideal for displaying carefully selected decorative objects. Adding a stenciled frieze in a geometric or stylized floral design was a popular method for introducing subtle detail to selected wall areas in original bungalows, and is a fairly easy, low-cost way to evoke the style in a contemporary home.

Linens in the Arts and Crafts era were handwoven and hand-embellished with simple motifs. Cross stitching, embroidery, and pulled-thread work frequently adorn table runners, chair cushions, and curtains. Curtains should produce a light and airy effect, welcoming sunlight into the home and allowing air to circulate freely. Today, the bungalow style once again makes use of such simple, natural fabrics for curtains and bedcovers as cotton, linen, or muslin, which drape easily and gently diffuse light.

One of the most collectible areas of Arts and Crafts material is art pottery, which provides lasting clues about the existence of many regional Arts and Crafts groups and local artistic traditions. While relatively vulnerable paintings and textiles have often disappeared, many pieces of sturdy decorative pottery remain near the kilns of their origin. So it is still possible to find Ariquipa pottery in Marin, California; Markham pottery near Ann Arbor, Michigan; and pieces from the famous Rookwood Pottery in Cincinnati, Ohio.

This pottery is most frequently of simple form and shape with matte glaze. Pots and vases were designed to be backdrops for floral displays, not to compete with the arrangements. As appreciation for bungalows grows, authentic pieces of Arts and Crafts pottery become much more expensive and difficult to find, but there are alternatives that work quite well in bungalow decors. Native American pots, with their warm earth tones and strong geometric patterns, are beautiful and fit well with the ideal of taking inspiration from nature.

now make excellent reproductions, as well as new designs that are quite suitable.

Another place to utilize reproductions is on the walls. The elaborately figured wallpaper of the Victorian home does not suit the bungalow aesthetic, but simpler motifs with colors derived from nature fit the look. Many of today's manufacturers sell reproductions of

OPPOSITE: *Today's bungalow enthusiast is very fortunate to have resources such as the wallpapers of Bradbury and Bradbury available for reproducing a period interior. This design firm, located in Benicia, California, has been a leader in re-creating both bungalow designs and bungalow values, since they make many of their papers by hand.*

ABOVE: *Simple objects, chosen for their inherent beauty and utility, are thoughtfully displayed along this polished wooden mantel. Copper pieces, decorative pottery, and the striking grain of the oak frames on the mirror and vintage photograph are displayed to great advantage against the warm, neutral background provided by the softly painted wall.*

ABOVE: *There are many high-quality reproductions of Craftsman furnishings available today. This clock is just one example of the beautiful pieces that can enhance a bungalow's decor. The casework is simple; the grain of the oak and the face of the clock itself provide the only decorative elements.*

ABOVE: *Hammered copper "bean pot" lamps with mica shades, designed by partners D'Arcy Gaw and Dirk Van Erp, are now highly prized by collectors of Arts and Crafts designs. These lamps have proven to be so popular that many reproductions are now available for buyers who like the look and feel of hammered copper but not the price of a museum-quality original.*

ABOVE: *The hand of the creator is evident in these unique Arts and Crafts—era accessories. The heavily embroidered linen tablecloth is a perfect example of the beautiful textiles found in the bungalow home. The teddy bear, which was named after Theodore Roosevelt, is an appropriate piece of whimsy, since this toy first became popular during the bungalow era.*

ABOVE: *Bungalow style lends itself well to eclectic interpretations. The details in this room recall the turn of the century, when the kerosene lamps and decorative molding of the Victorian era were combined with wicker, naturally finished woods, and Japanese elements, such as this beautiful antique chest.*

OPPOSITE: *It is not necessary to search long and hard for decorative items to accessorize a bungalow-style room. Here, an antique desk, a glorious garden, and the colorful bindings of the library provide all the decorative interest necessary.*

OPPOSITE: *The warm, neutral wall treatment is the perfect backdrop for this little Arts and Crafts desk made of oak. The back of the oak chair and the side of the desk share similar detailing. The floral motif of the picture frame is echoed in the art pottery jug atop the desk and the inlays on the desk itself.*

ABOVE: *Wallpaper with botanical motifs in soft, natural colors, such as this one in a design inspired by William Morris, are the perfect backdrop for bungalow furnishings. Here, an oak chair and end table in the Craftsman style complete the period setting.*

LEFT, TOP: *Careful to avoid frills and extraneous adornments, bungalow decor involves a great deal of consideration in its design. Here, fresh field flowers are arranged in mason jars that are still in their canning rack, creating a nice mix of the utilitarian and the decorative. As this illustrates, there is often only a fine line between bungalow style and cottage style.*

LEFT, BOTTOM: *In the bungalow aesthetic, every opportunity is taken to enjoy natural beauty. The generous window in this breakfast nook opens onto a sunny, tree-filled yard, and a bunch of flowers fresh from the garden enhances the connection with the outdoors.*

OPPOSITE: *The symmetry of the three pairs of cupboard doors, with their striking use of glass, is a subtle design element in this eat-in kitchen. Fine craftsmanship is a hallmark of the Arts and Crafts Movement, and beautifully designed built-ins are found in many bungalows.*

OPPOSITE: *This contemporary interpretation of the light, airy bungalow bedroom includes translucent curtains and cotton bed linens that are pale and soothing. Furnishings are kept to a minimum for a simple, uncluttered look; an attractive iron bed and a small table are all that's needed.*

ABOVE, LEFT: *The woodland scenery is an important decorative element in this bedroom: note how the curtains and louvers can be opened to allow the natural beauty of the trees to be seen. The neutral palette of the vintage dresser, the matelassé bedspread, and the patchwork quilt with its matching pillow complement the nature theme.*

ABOVE, RIGHT: *Cool, restful colors are traditional for the sleeping rooms in bungalows. Woodwork is usually painted white or a very light color. The vibrant robin's-egg blue used on the walls in this bedroom points to a modern take on the style, but the white linens and extremely simple furniture are a nod to the bungalow's past.*

LEFT: *This bungalow celebrates comfort by the fireside with its clean-lined overstuffed chair and its warm palette of autumnal hues. The color scheme extends to details like the book bindings and flowers, creating an atmosphere of security and contentment.*

OPPOSITE: *Bungalow style covers a wide range of interior decor, from the workingman's cottage with its homemade furniture to the completely integrated interiors and furniture of the Greene brothers. This bungalow has the rustic charm of a Colonial-era home.*

CHAPTER FOUR

LIVING WITH NATURE: THE BUNGALOW GARDEN

The Arts and Crafts Movement celebrated an important relationship between humans and nature. Understanding nature was seen as the path to inner peace, a way to find balance and harmony in an imperfect world. The gardens of the bungalow era are especially noteworthy because they were created with the underlying philosophy of finding one's spirit through the contemplation of nature.

Formal lawns with neat borders of box hedges and carefully colored beds of spectacular florals are not suited to the bungalow garden. As informality and spontaneity became design considerations, the elaborate birdbath of the Victorian age gave way to the understated reflecting pool. Now a simple, natural garden could be created around an especially interesting tree. A gnarled pine, a grove of birches, or a sturdy old oak often became the focal point for the garden setting.

Porches and verandahs are prominent features of many bungalows and have always been important living areas, especially during the summer months. Sitting in the sunshine, especially during the winter, was considered a healthy practice. The front porch became more than just a place to find one's latchkey; it was now a room in which to rest or to entertain friends. When situated on the south and east sides of the house, the wraparound porch provided sunny comfort on winter mornings and a cool place to sit on warm summer afternoons.

The porch usually had its own furniture, such as lightweight and airy chairs and settees made of wicker or rattan. Sometimes a swing or a hammock graced the porch. Informal tables provided places for playing checkers or cards, and there might be a rocking chair or two and occasionally a cot. Floor coverings, if any, were thin grass or sisal mats. Cushions on the chairs and chaises were made of weather-resistant fabric, such as canvas or duck. Porch living is nearly the same today. Lightweight furniture appears as soon as the weather is warm enough, sisal mats cover the floor, and clean canvas dresses chairs and chaises. Porch furniture from the bungalow era can still frequently be found at garage sales. It is much more interesting than the molded resin chairs available today and often just as inexpensive.

The gardens discussed in the early writings of the great Arts and Crafts philosophers seem to follow two very different design

OPPOSITE: *Bungalows generally have large, overhanging eaves to shade the house from strong sunlight. The eaves are relatively shallow at the front of this house, where a table and chairs provide a spot for an alfresco meal, but they are extended as a trellis at the side of the building, providing still another opportunity to enjoy the garden.*

schemes. Sometimes the house is sited to take advantage of the view and the existing trees and foliage. The emphasis in this approach is on the appreciation and preservation of the natural environment. The landscape immediately around the house may be enhanced with native flowers and plants, but great care is taken to leave natural beauty undisturbed.

The second scheme is to create a garden around the house that includes plants that exhilarate the soul and captivate the senses, such as sweet William, columbine, poppies, asters, and foxgloves. This approach requires that the garden be viewed as a work of art, with the gardener taking as much care with color and composition as any landscape painter.

These two design philosophies would seem to be complete opposites, but they do have a common link: the landscape, whether natural or man-made, should affect the spirit. The garden should be integral to the house and both should be places of comfort and repose. The front walkway should prepare the resident or visitor for the transition from the outside world to the shelter of the home.

One of the benefits of acquiring an older bungalow is that a mature landscape comes with it, one where the trees and shrubs have reached their full height. Today's bungalow gardener generally maintains the old traditions, planting favorite perennials and native flowers where they will be enjoyed most. Those who build new bungalows often appreciate the informal, low-maintenance landscaping that is part of the bungalow style, but they are not limited by strict rules. Rather, the modern bungalow gardener is guided by his or her own preferences. A meditation area, a butterfly garden, a wildlife habitat or a protected ecosystem—all of these types of gardens are perfectly consistent with the bungalow philosophy of living with nature.

BELOW: *The rock wall leading up to this bungalow has been softened with plantings of native flowers. Covered with shingles and surrounded with a colorful garden, the home seems cozy and inviting despite its imposing site.*

OPPOSITE: *The porch of a bungalow often takes the place of the living room during the summer months, since it is the perfect place for families and friends to sit and visit. This lovely porch has plenty of shade, a wind chime that provides peaceful music when the wind blows, and beautiful hydrangeas to please the eye.*

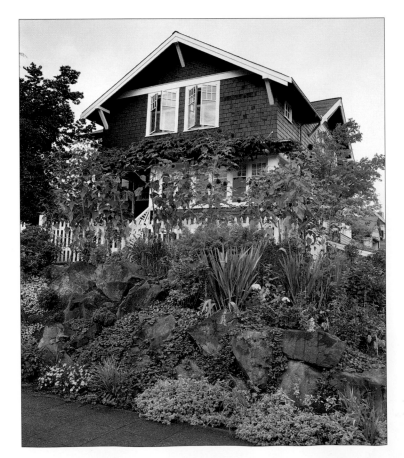

OPPOSITE:

Outdoor dining is delightful in warm weather, and many bungalow porches hold a small table and chairs. Carpeting such as this reed matting is especially suitable to the porch, creating an inviting space for family meals during those barefoot months of summer.

RIGHT: *Is there a better way to enjoy the outdoors than sitting under trees laden with ripe fruit? Sometimes a deck can be built as an extension of the porch, to increase outdoor living space. This one has been allowed to weather to a silvery gray to complement the setting.*

ABOVE: *Sitting in the garden and contemplating the landscape is a path to composure and inner harmony.*
Rustic furniture, like this twig settee, invites one to take the time to relax in the sun and listen to the birds.

ABOVE: *A cozy corner on the back porch of this bungalow offers a place to sit in the sun and visit with friends. Solid Craftsman-style outdoor furnishings, such as this table and chairs, are now available from a number of suppliers. White paint and cheery striped cushions make the traditional design feel contemporary.*

LEFT: *The sound of water trickling and splashing is especially restful. In a contemplative garden, or even in an interior courtyard such as this, a pool can be an important feature for calming the soul.*

ABOVE: *A simple pergola over the garden gate, crafted in the bungalow style, urges visitors to leave the busy workaday world outside, for this is a place of quiet and repose. The small porch light hanging from the eaves is typical of Arts and Crafts design, simply yet beautifully made.*

ABOVE: *Porch life calls for comfortable chairs and a railing on which to rest one's feet. A swing is always a wonderful addition if there is enough room. On this comfortable porch, a magnificent tree trunk is the focal element, shading the house and offering some privacy from the street.*

OPPOSITE: *Porch furniture comes in a wide variety of styles and materials. One traditional type is the pierced metal chair, such as these vintage examples. Be sure to provide cushions, since these seats can be either very hot or very cold, depending on the weather.*

ABOVE: *The generous windows of this prairie-style bungalow offer another opportunity to bring the outdoors inside. Only a step or two separates the homeowner from the garden, which contains a cheerful assortment of favorite flowers.*

ABOVE: *The unspoiled vista was an important consideration in the construction of the traditional bungalow. Bungalows were sited to take advantage of spectacular views—as this one certainly does—to bring nature indoors in every season. The owner has created a garden indoors by placing clusters of potted plants around the table.*

LEFT: *The typical bungalow garden follows one of two completely opposing philosophies. One seeks to preserve the natural setting, the other to pull natural beauty into the living space. This small garden falls into the second category, with its trellis of roses and beds of irises and other favorite flowers planted right against the bungalow's walls.*

A B O V E : *This vintage bungalow, with its redwood shingles and tidy white trim, was built before World War I.*
The small porch is perfect for sitting and enjoying the sights and scents of the nearby flowers. The modest home is
set off by a thoughtfully detailed fence and arbor, providing an invitation to passersby to slow down and enjoy the
tranquil harmony of the house and garden.

PHOTO CREDITS

©Laurie Black: pp. 59 top, 62, 74 bottom; p. 59 bottom (architect: Gregory J. Bader Architects, Seattle, WA); p. 46 (designer: Suzi Andersson Blucher, the New Kitchen, Eugene, OR); pp. 8, 27, 93 (architect: Mike Dowd, Portland, OR); pp. 52, 77 left (designer: Ellen Dupps, Hilton Head, S.C.); p. 47 (designer: John Hurst, Eugene, OR); pp. 5, 41, 63 right, 77 right, 78 (designer: Bradley Huson, Seattle, WA; architect: Barb Christensen, Seattle, WA); pp. 34, 85 (designer: Julia Lundy Associates, Portland, OR); pp. 53, 60, 82 (designer: M. Paige Mitchell Interior Design, Seattle, WA); p. 43 (designer: Beth Robley Design, Portland, OR; architect: Mike Dowd, Portland, OR)

Esto: ©Mark Darley: pp. 29 (architects: Turnbull, Griffin, Haesloop Architects); ©Jeff Goldberg: pp.10-11 (architects: Centerbrook Architects)

©Anne Gumerson: p. 50 (architect: Sarah Schweitzer/SMDA Architects of Baltimore)

©April Halberstadt: pp. 21 bottom, 28, 30 top, 32

©Hans Halberstadt: p. 68 left

©Michael Jensen: pp. 12, 30 bottom, 35 top, 87; pp. 26, 45, 48, 51 (architect: Tom Bosworth); pp. 70, 75 (designer: Anne Fisher); p. 76 (designer: Tarsi Pantages); p. 58 (designer: Roberta Root)

Private Collection: pp. 2, 7, 13, 15, 16, 18-19, 20, 21 top, 23, 24-25, 31, 33, 39, 44, 49, 55 right, 56, 63 left, 66, 67, 68 right, 69, 73, 83, 86, 89 right, 90, 94, 95

©Brad Simmons: pp. 35 bottom, 40, 61, 74 top, 79, 84, 91

©Tim Street-Porter: pp. 64; pp. 14, 42, 57, 72 (Gamble House, architects: Greene & Greene) pp. 36, 54-55, 88-89 (Irwin House, architects: Greene & Greene)

Elizabeth Whiting Associates: pp. 22, 71, 80, 92